EXPLORING SCIENCE

by Roger Hurt
designed and illustrated by Stuart Trotter

Ladybird Books

What about us?

Look at these children. What can you see that is similar and different? Some things are obvious, others are not!

We have recorded some of their personal facts on this chart...

	GIRL?	BLUE EYES?	BROWN HAIR?	SWIM 200 m?	HAS A PET?	RIGHT HANDED?	TALLER THAN 1.50 m?
Ann	✓		✓				
Jim		✓				✓	✓
Pete						✓	
Angus				✓		✓	✓
Lyn	✓		✓	✓	✓	✓	✓
							✓

PERSONAL DATA is another phrase for information about ourselves. There is a better way to store this DATA so that we can read it more quickly. We need some cards made like this...

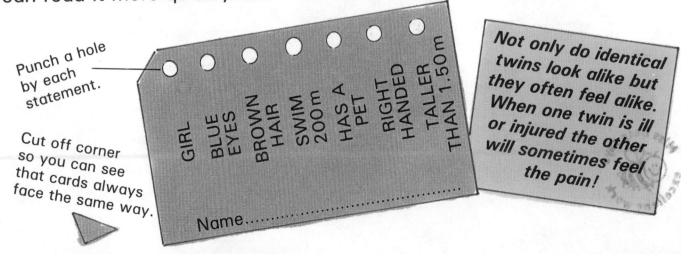

Punch a hole by each statement.

Cut off corner so you can see that cards always face the same way.

GIRL BLUE EYES BROWN HAIR SWIM 200 m HAS A PET RIGHT HANDED TALLER THAN 1.50 m

Name.....................

Not only do identical twins look alike but they often feel alike. When one twin is ill or injured the other will sometimes feel the pain!

Collect this personal data from lots of people. If the answer to a question is **no** then cut the hole into a slot, like these...

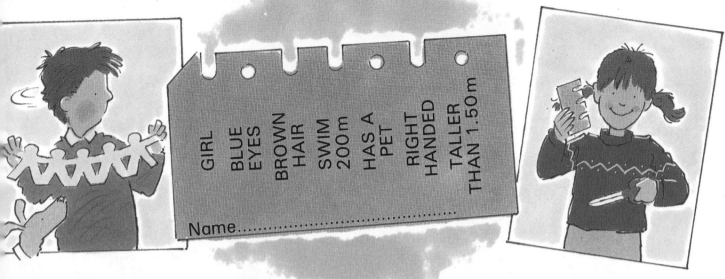

The card reads, with columns labelled: GIRL, BLUE EYES, BROWN HAIR, SWIM 200m, HAS A PET, RIGHT HANDED, TALLER THAN 1.50m. Name........

Now we have a DATA BANK on you and your friends and we can **interrogate** it like this: if we want to find which of our friends has a pet we can put a knitting needle through the hole marked HAS A PET, and by gently lifting the cards up only the friends with pets will be selected.

You can also ask two questions or more. Find out which of your friends are good swimmers *and* have blue eyes! Try other combinations.

knitting needles

Early computers used a similar method to store information. Like our DATA BANK all the questions have to be able to be answered with a yes or no.

Acids and alkalis

Acids and alkalis are important groups of chemicals. Acids are sour and give us, for instance, the sharp taste in a lemon. Alkalis are bitter. Scientists use **litmus paper** to test if a substance is acid or alkaline.

You can make your own testing agent. Cut a red cabbage into thin strips and pour boiling water over them. Leave this to cool, then strain off the purple coloured liquid into a jar.

Put small amounts of the following onto saucers: coffee, orange squash, water, toothpaste, earth, vinegar, tea and scouring powder. Now test each substance by dropping small amounts of the cabbage liquid onto it. If the liquid turns red the substance is an acid and if it turns blue the substance is an alkali.

Make a chart and record the results. Try testing some of your saliva!

	ACID	ALKALI
coffee		
earth		
tea		

Keep it warm

Put equal amounts of hot water in four identical margarine tubs. Replace the lids and do the following:

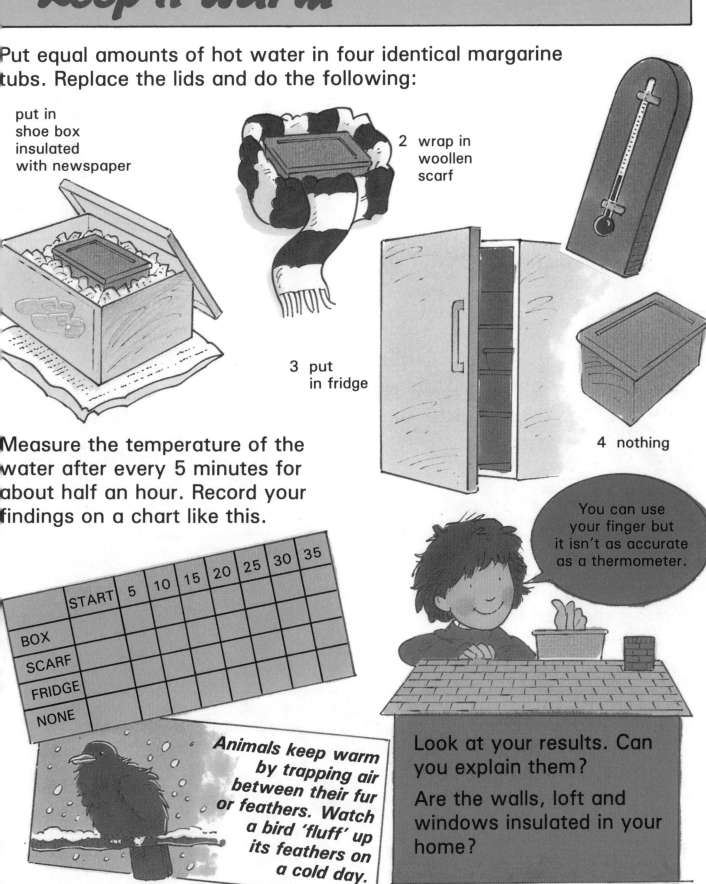

put in shoe box insulated with newspaper

2 wrap in woollen scarf

3 put in fridge

4 nothing

Measure the temperature of the water after every 5 minutes for about half an hour. Record your findings on a chart like this.

	START	5	10	15	20	25	30	35
BOX								
SCARF								
FRIDGE								
NONE								

You can use your finger but it isn't as accurate as a thermometer.

Animals keep warm by trapping air between their fur or feathers. Watch a bird 'fluff' up its feathers on a cold day.

Look at your results. Can you explain them?

Are the walls, loft and windows insulated in your home?

Test your senses

We have five **senses** which help us to be aware of what is going on around us. These are **touch**, **taste**, **sight**, **smell** and **hearing**.

Collect five everyday objects of different sizes and shapes.

Put them in a pillowcase and get a friend to identify each object by using *touch* alone.

Foxes have an amazing sense of smell. They can smell water from over a kilometer away, even when there is a rubbish tip in the way!

Your fingers are very sensitive and can feel irregularities of less than 0.1mm!

Find out about Braille and just how blind people can read in bed and still keep their arms warm!

Collect the following: salt, sugar, lemon juice, vinegar and flour. Put each one in a small container and number them. Now get a friend to see if they can identify them by *smell* alone.

Next carefully *taste* each substance to see if you or your friend has the better sense of smell and taste!

The senses of taste and smell are very closely linked, which is why we don't enjoy the taste of food so much when we have a cold.

Make your own eye chart on a big piece of paper. It is important to remember that this is NOT a real eye test.

Pin your chart to a wall and try to read the letters from 5 m away, first with one eye and then the other and finally with both.

Do you notice a difference? Is one eye better than the other?

Can you hear a pin drop? This is one way to test your *hearing*. Find a metal tray and a large pin. Ask a friend to drop the pin onto the tray from a height of 30 cm, while your back is turned. Can you hear the noise? Now move further and further away until you can't hear the sound.

If we lose one of our senses, for example going blind, then the other four often improve to make up for the loss!

What a load of rot

One of the great environmental problems we have today is that we make too much rubbish. Some rubbish does not rot away. We say it is **non-biodegradable**.

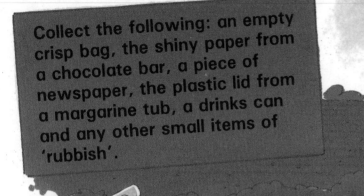

Collect the following: an empty crisp bag, the shiny paper from a chocolate bar, a piece of newspaper, the plastic lid from a margarine tub, a drinks can and any other small items of 'rubbish'.

In a spare part of your garden bury the items under about 15 cm of soil.

Water the soil every day (no, they won't grow!) and after two weeks have a look. Has there been any great change in the objects. If you had waited two months would there have been a greater change?

Some rubbish can be **re-cycled**, that is, used again. Start an aluminium can collection.

Cans can be tested with a magnet. If the magnet does NOT stick to the can then it is aluminium and worth money!

Do you have the solution?

Some substances are **soluble**, that is they dissolve in water. Others are not. Find out which of the following are soluble.

You will need one teaspoon of each of the following: sugar, sand, salt, curry powder and chalk (crush a stick).

SOLUBLE	✓ or ✗
SUGAR 1	
SAND 2	
SALT 3	
CURRY 4	
CHALK 5	

Now find five clean empty jam jars with lids and label them 1 to 5. Half fill them with warm water and put a different substance in each one. Put the lids on and shake each one for 30 seconds.

Does any of the original substance remain? Record your findings on a chart like ours.

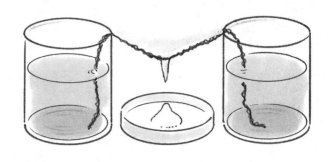

Have you ever been in a cave or pothole? You may have seen **stalactites** and **stalagmites**. Here's how to make your own!

Mix a solution of washing soda in two jars until no more soda will dissolve. Hang string in them as shown and wait for a few days. You should begin to have a stalactite and stalagmite of your own!

How do you remember which is which? StalacTites Trickle down. StalagMites Mount up.

Think about friction

Friction is the force that makes things 'grip' each other. Without it we would not be able to walk, ride a bike or climb a tree. Some things have more 'grip' or friction than others.

Make a friction tester like this...

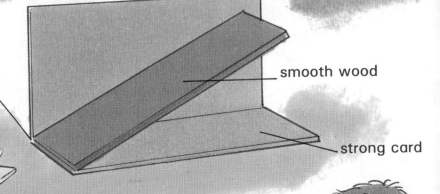

hinge joined with insulating tape or sticking plaster

smooth wood

strong card

Wrap a block of wood in different coverings in turn. For example, polythene, newspaper, an old sock, sandpaper, a handkerchief and an old innertube.

Place the block at the top of the friction tester and slowly start to tilt the wooden surface. When the block slides down the slope, mark the angle on the card.

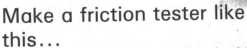
sandpaper

Now repeat the experiment with the other coverings. Could you have estimated which covering would grip better than others?

When you skate on ice there is little friction because your weight melts the ice and you are in fact skating on a film of water!

Let's bake

You may think baking bread is not a real scientific experiment. But the action of sugar on yeast is a **chemical reaction**. (Anyway fresh bread is always good to eat!)

You will need:
250 gms of strong white or wholewheat flour
1 teaspoon of butter
1 teaspoon of sugar
2 teaspoons of salt
2 teaspoons dried yeast
125 ml of hand-hot water

1 Mix the flour, salt and butter in a large bowl and leave in a warm place.

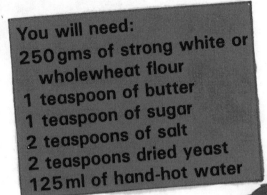

2 Sprinkle the yeast and sugar onto the warm water, stir well and set aside until 2 cm of frothy 'head' has formed.

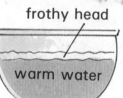

frothy head

warm water

3 Pour the yeast mixture into the flour mixture. Stir with a wooden spoon and then mix with your hands. Put the dough, as it is now called, onto a flat surface and knead for about 5 minutes. It should become quite elastic and springy...

4 Divide the dough into 6 rolls and place them on a well-greased baking tray. Cover with a clean tea towel and leave for about an hour.

5 Put the bread into an oven that has been pre-heated to Gas mark 7 or 220°C (you may need an adult to help here) and bake for 20-25 minutes. The bread should sound hollow when tapped.

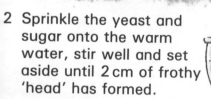

The head is caused by carbon dioxide (CO_2) being given off by the action of the sugar on the yeast.

When you leave your small rolls for an hour the yeast is working again and the CO_2 is making the rolls twice their size with the little 'air' holes you always see in bread.

Yeast is also used in making beer and wine!

Whatever the weather

Collecting weather records is always interesting and the older you get the more accurate your records and your equipment can become.

RAIN GAUGE

You will need an empty, clear plastic bottle with a flat bottom. Cut off the top and fit it upside down into the rest of the bottle.

Place your gauge outside, not too near a building.

Use a ruler with millimetres and record the rainfall every day.

Don't forget to empty your gauge if it has rained!

AIR PRESSURE

This affects the weather. The lines you see on a weather chart show the different areas of high or low pressure.
Make a simple **barometer**, the instrument used for measuring air pressure.

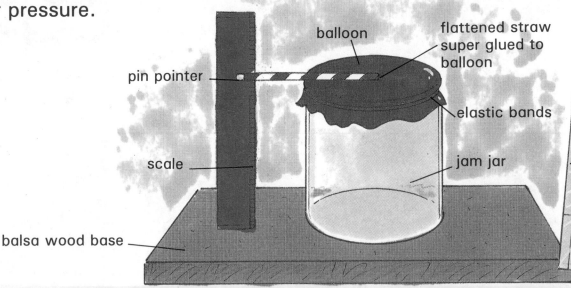

pin pointer

balloon

flattened straw super glued to balloon

elastic bands

scale

jam jar

balsa wood base

This doesn't give very accurate readings but you can use it to compare air pressure from one day to the next. Record your readings each day.

Colours

Most colours are made by mixing other colours. We need only three colours to produce all the other colours.

These are RED, YELLOW, and BLUE and they are called the PRIMARY COLOURS.

When we mix these colours in pairs the results are called SECONDARY COLOURS.

Sunlight looks colourless and is called **white light**. But it is in fact made up from all the colours of the **spectrum**. These are **R**ed, **O**range, **Y**ellow, **G**reen, **B**lue, **I**ndigo and **V**iolet. You can remember these colours and their order by saying the phrase: **R**ichard **O**f **Y**ork **G**ained **B**attles **I**n **V**ain.

When we see a colour it is because the material we are looking at absorbs some colours and reflects others.

This red shirt is reflecting red light and absorbing the other colours in white light. The black shorts look black because they are absorbing all the colours of white light.

Some people are not able to see colours as well as others. These people have a colour deficiency and are sometimes called 'colour blind'. The most common form is a red-green deficiency. About 1 in every 16 males is colour blind while only 1 in 100 females is affected!

Now let's make some colour mixers. Carefully cut out the coloured circles and make a hole in the centre. Then push a small (5 cm) six-sided pencil through the hole.

Spin the disc and the colours will mix. This disc has the colours of the spectrum and you should see **white light**.

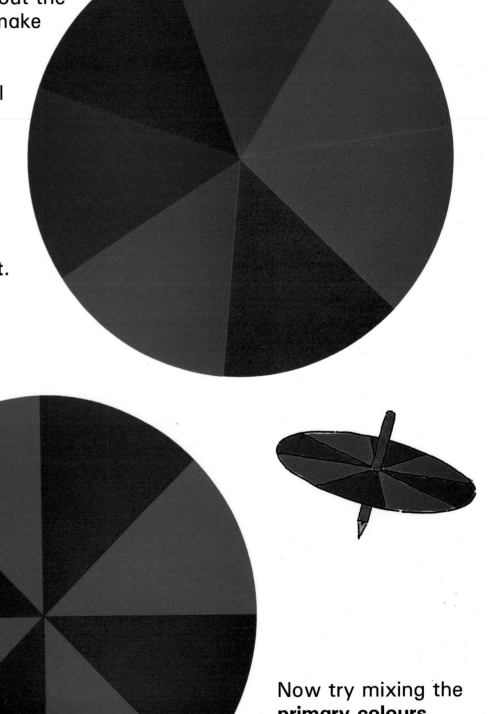

Now try mixing the **primary colours**. Make a note of the colours you see when you spin the discs.

Now try these.

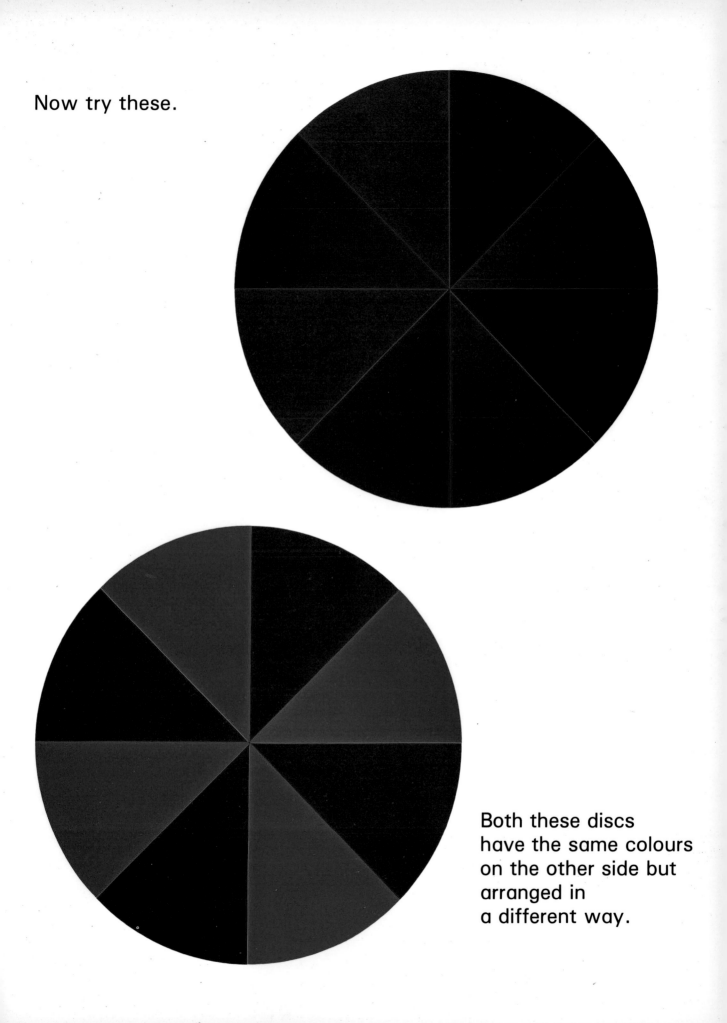

Both these discs
have the same colours
on the other side but
arranged in
a different way.

Did this arrangement
make a better
mix or not? Can you
explain why?

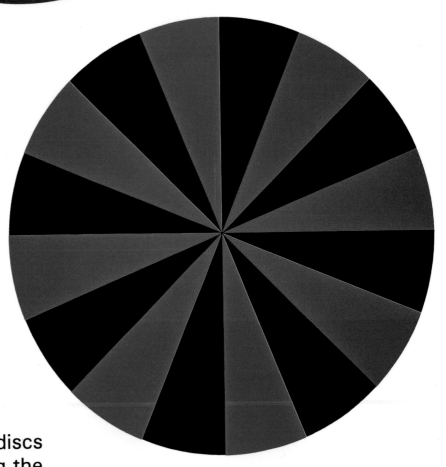

Now try making some discs
of your own and mixing the
secondary colours.

WIND

There are two things we need to know. How strong the wind is blowing and in what direction. Try making a simple **anemometer** (wind speed indicator).

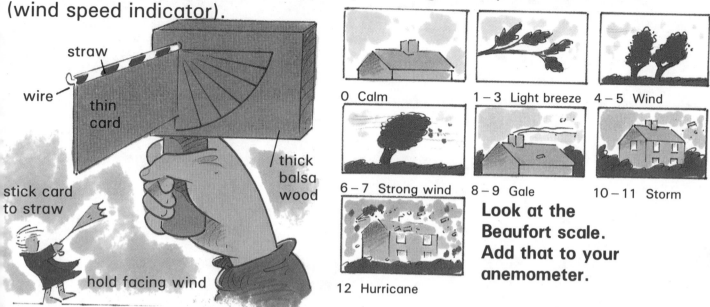

straw

wire

thin card

thick balsa wood

stick card to straw

hold facing wind

0 Calm

1 – 3 Light breeze

4 – 5 Wind

6 – 7 Strong wind

8 – 9 Gale

10 – 11 Storm

12 Hurricane

Look at the Beaufort scale. Add that to your anemometer.

You will be able to record your own wind speed number and compare it from day to day.

Weather vanes show wind direction. They are fun to make and can be different shapes and sizes provided you follow a few simple rules. Here is one way to make a weather vane.

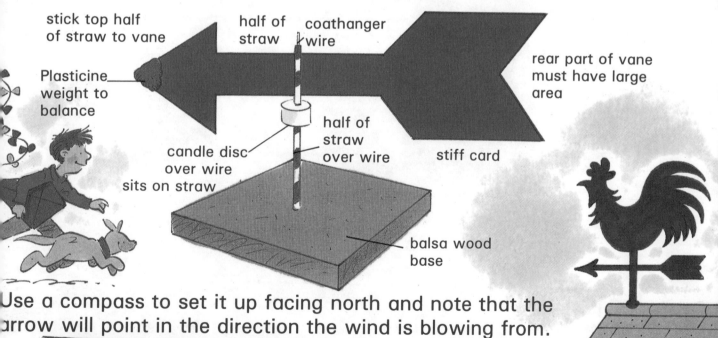

stick top half of straw to vane

half of straw

coathanger wire

rear part of vane must have large area

Plasticine weight to balance

candle disc over wire sits on straw

half of straw over wire

stiff card

balsa wood base

Use a compass to set it up facing north and note that the arrow will point in the direction the wind is blowing from.

Weather vanes can give a clue to what sort of people live nearby. Have you seen huntsmen or cricketers on roofs? The most common weather vane is in the shape of a cockerel.

Electrician's shorthand

There are many exciting experiments you can do with electricity BUT you must NEVER use mains electricity. This is at 240 volts. You will only need 4.5 volt batteries.
NEVER play with a car battery. It contains acid and is dangerous.

You will already have learned how to make a bulb light using a simple circuit like this...

You can also make a circuit with a switch like this.

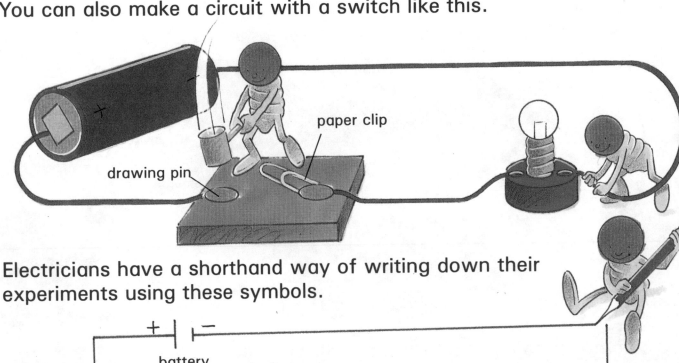

Electricians have a shorthand way of writing down their experiments using these symbols.

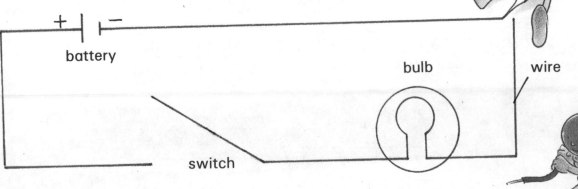

Now wire up bulbs **in parallel** like this.

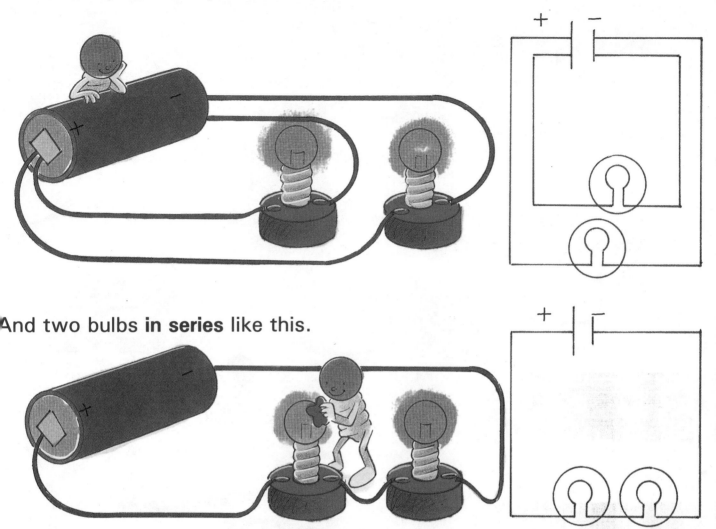

And two bulbs **in series** like this.

Do you notice a difference in the brightness of the bulbs?
Can you explain this?

The bulbs *in series* are having to 'share' the power from the battery whilst the bulbs *in parallel* are getting their own supply via their own wires.

Follow this electrician's diagram. What could you make with this circuit?

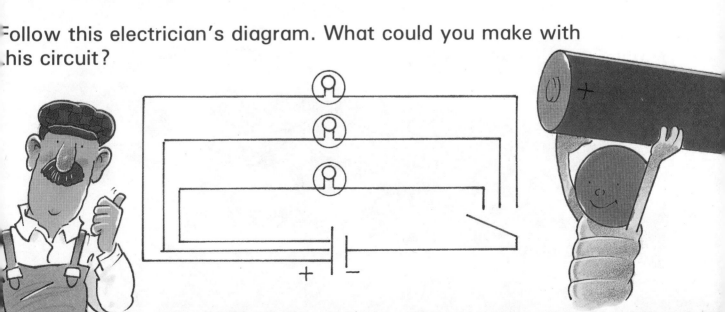

More electrics!

Some materials are able to carry electricity, some are not. Make a tester like this...

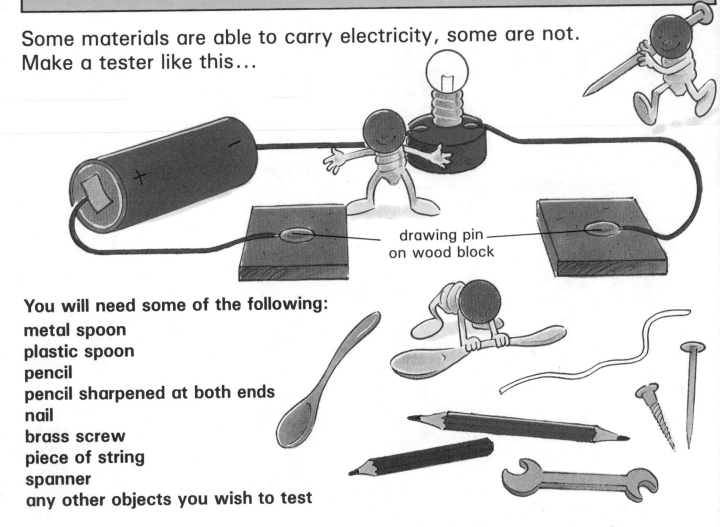

drawing pin on wood block

You will need some of the following:
metal spoon
plastic spoon
pencil
pencil sharpened at both ends
nail
brass screw
piece of string
spanner
any other objects you wish to test

In turn, place the objects across the **terminals** (the two drawing pins) and see if electricity travels along them and lights up the bulb.

Record your findings on a chart with a tick or cross. If the bulb does light up we say that the object placed across the terminals **conducts** electricity.

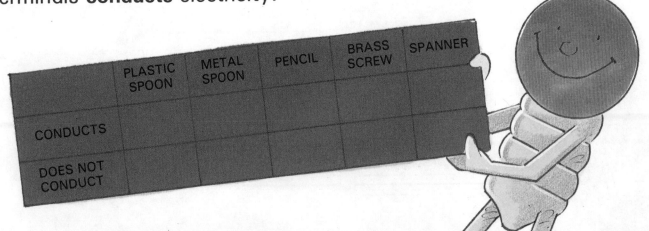

	PLASTIC SPOON	METAL SPOON	PENCIL	BRASS SCREW	SPANNER
CONDUCTS					
DOES NOT CONDUCT					

You can make your own **electromagnet**. You will need a length of wire, a large nail and two batteries joined together (electromagnets use plenty of power).

Make the circuit like this.

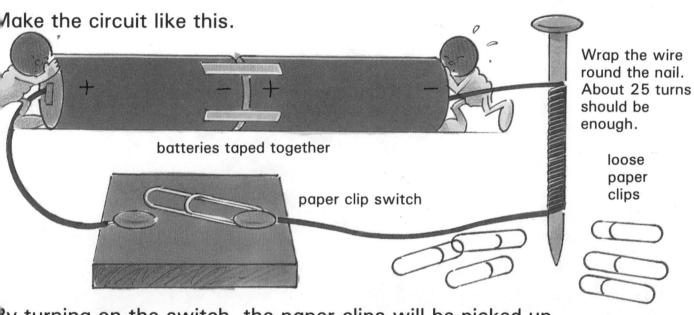

batteries taped together

paper clip switch

Wrap the wire round the nail. About 25 turns should be enough.

loose paper clips

By turning on the switch, the paper clips will be picked up. They will fall off when the switch is turned off.

Count how many paper clips are picked up. Now try 50 turns of wire and repeat the experiment.

Then try adding another battery with both 25 and 50 turns. Record your findings on a chart like this.

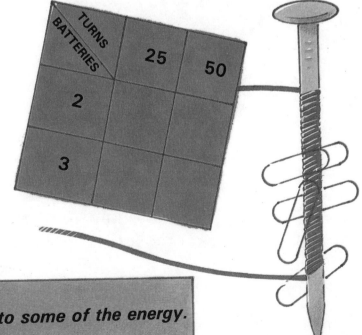

TURNS / BATTERIES	25	50
2		
3		

Did the wire get warm?
Now you know what happens to some of the energy.

When you blow up a balloon you are forcing air, under pressure, into the thin skin of the balloon. This air is a form of **stored energy** and when released, it can power a variety of 'vehicles'.

Rocket

straw

thread strin through str and pull tig

Sellotape straw to blown-up balloon

Rocket Car

Sellotape blown-up balloon to wheel base

You could make the wheel base from Meccano™ or Lego™.

Hovercraft

balloon neck pushed through hole of large plastic lid

When you release the air it will escape very quickly and the 'rocket' will soon come to a halt. You can slow down the escaping air by filling the mouth of the balloon with Plasticine and then making a smaller hole with a thin nail.

These are not proper jet engines. The first jet engine was invented in 1930 by Sir Frank Whittle. See what you can find out about him.

A lot of hot air!

Hot air always rises. You can use this effect to help you fly a hot air balloon!

You will need a large but very light bag. A thin plastic bin liner is ideal. Fix this bag to a light wire frame (the wire used by flower arrangers will do fine.)

Try to use as little glue or Sellotape as possible to keep the balloon light.

The best way to fill the balloon with hot air is to use a hair dryer.

hair dryer

The first successful human flight was in a hot air balloon. The designers were the Montgolfier brothers. Their balloon flew in France in 1783.

You will find that your balloon will work far better on a cold day as the difference in the temperature inside the balloon and outside the balloon will be greater.

Travelling light

Light always travels in straight lines. The only way we can 'bend' light is by **reflecting** it. Mirrors are some of the best reflectors.

Make a periscope

You will need a cardboard tube (a kitchen roll inner will do) and two small mirrors. (It's a good idea to protect the edges of the mirrors with tape.)

Cut the tube, as shown, with a craft knife or junior hacksaw. ***Ask an adult to help***. The angle of cut for the mirrors is important as is shown in the diagram.

Can you make a 'scope' to see what is going on behind you? What are you going to call this instrument?

45°

45°

mirrors here

Periscopes are not only used in submarines, they were used in the First World War to see over the top of trenches safely! You can use yours to see over the top of a crowd.

or many years scientists have made pin-hole viewers in order
show that light travels in a straight line.

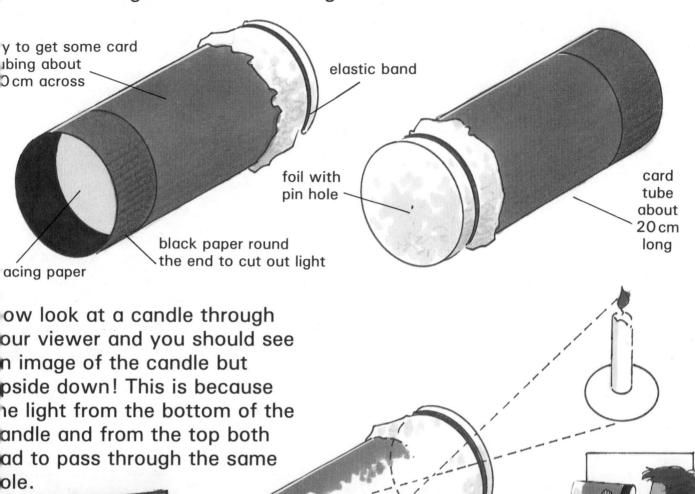

y to get some card
ubing about
0 cm across

elastic band

foil with
pin hole

card
tube
about
20 cm
long

black paper round
the end to cut out light

tracing paper

ow look at a candle through
our viewer and you should see
n image of the candle but
pside down! This is because
he light from the bottom of the
andle and from the top both
ad to pass through the same
ole.

The early cameras
worked like this
except the tracing
paper was replaced
with photographic
paper.

You may have to experiment with
the size of hole – a larger hole
makes the image brighter but less
sharp.

Do you know that light travels
at 300,000,000 m per
second, light from the sun
takes around 8 minutes
to reach earth. Sound
travels much more slowly at
around 340 m per second.
This is why we see lightning
before we hear thunder.

Sounds good

Sounds are made by **vibrations**. We have two bands of cartilage in our larynx (in the throat) which vibrate when we push air past them. The faster they vibrate the higher our voice.

All instruments make their sounds by vibrations of different types.

aagh!

The notes on a guitar are altered in two ways: either by turning the pegs or by holding a finger on a fret. We can reproduce these two effects.

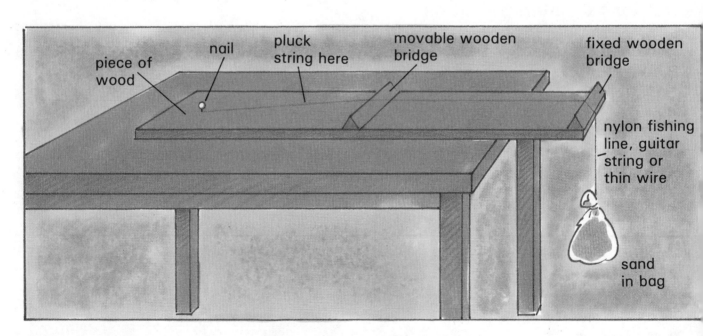

piece of wood

nail

pluck string here

movable wooden bridge

fixed wooden bridge

nylon fishing line, guitar string or thin wire

sand in bag

The heavier the weight, the higher the note, just like turning the pegs.

Moving the bridge is like holding the string on a fret.

Experiment with different weights and different string lengths and see what sounds you can get!

Sounds better

Have you ever tapped a glass bottle containing water? You'll have noticed that you produce a note. Use this to make a musical instrument.

Collect eight identical bottles or jars. By putting different amounts of water in each bottle you can, with a little experimentation, produce a scale – **Doh, Ray, Me, Fah, Soh, Lah, Tee** and **Doh**. By tapping the bottles gently with a spoon you should be able to play a simple tune.

Remember, don't get too enthusiastic when you play your instrument. It is made of glass and can break!

What is vibrating to make the sound? Is it the water? In fact it's the air in the bottle. The more water we put in, the less room there is for the air to vibrate so it vibrates faster and makes a higher note.

Give yourself a test

1 What type of chemical gives the sour taste in lemons?

2 How do birds and other animals keep warm in winter?

3 Which sense does a fox possess that is especially keen?

4 What is the scientific name for material that will not rot?

6 What do ice skaters *actually* skate on?

5 Do stalactites grow up or down?

7 What gas is given off when sugar reacts with yeast?

8 Do you know the name of the scale used to measure wind speed?

9 What word do we use to say that a material carries electricity?

10 What do we call a vehicle that floats on a cushion of air?